Tell Me Something

Madison Bauer

A bit over a year of time

Can you blame me for sinking slowly
Into the depths of my own consciousness?
And yet I bite the lip of these words—
Oh, maybe I shall write, with this abbreviated breath
And maybe you'll see the ink drops
    And the errors
       And the smudges
Maybe you'll even fall in love with them.
But if you don't,
The truth is that I love them myself—
Is that not what you hate to hear?
That your love, though sweet,
Is like cotton candy
That melts the longer you hold it under your tongue.
For they said that men want women
Lovely and fragile, like glass
Transparent and breakable—
Pity.
I am steel,
Made from mills of flame and passion
And the words of my iron pen
Will too remain heavy on your chest;
So ask me now, reader,
Whether or not I know what I can do with them.

If you were to look for me
I'm sure you could find me,
But I wouldn't want you to—
I'd want you to tear apart the room
Pulling drawers from their sockets
As if what's inside holds the vision of me,
Mockingly quiet, far from reach;
In this dream it'd be fruitless, no trace of me left.

And yet here I am hidden in the closet, like a child,
The first place you'd look if you tried,
I wait when I hear you count to ten
As if it's a game—as if I can show myself
Like hide and seek;
Eyes closed, I run backwards
Underneath tables and behind curtains
Of a doll house, where faucets and locks are just for show.

You're like a rope
That pulls fast
And releases quick.

You brush my skin
But the scratch comes later—
The pain's trace tardy.

Yes, I can feel you
Closing in now—
My face reddens.

There's little air left
But you pinch the fear
With every word I choke.

Oh, this is your finale
As you silence me
On the branch of a tree.

You will have no possession over me now,
I'll slip through your fingers
Like fraudulent grains of sand
Wanting to be whole
And free
And alive;
I hate feeling half-dead
With bits of myself
Floating in other people's pockets,
And so I'll turn them inside out,
Looking for change.

Everything dissolves,
Even that which loomed over our heads
Will become craters in the earth
With each passing of the sun—

    But what of these unsaid words,
    Who denies their grudge?
    Smothered by these pages,
    They will exist on and on
    Mumbling even when I'm left to bones,
    Perennial plants rising from the grass above me.

I room ticks, I lie—
Awake and frozen, like the undead
Eternal men, paved into carbonite
Longing to move bodies
That feel like corpses—
Do they beg for time to pass,
Or stand still?
Are they alive
If they are stuck in time,
Free from rot,
But waiting for the hand
To reach into the freezer
And stick them into a microwave?
Night, pass!

I think there is a feeling
That boils somewhere within
And spills over the sides
When no one speaks.

I feel the steam climbing up, up
My throat swells with the pressure
Fingers twitching at the heat—
They redden, they burn.

Lonely cliffs sing of past loves
Echoing the succulent past
From a poet's lips
Dipped in honey.

That sweet nectar
So delicious,
It stings
With the malice of bees.

I am here again
I remember the feeling;
There is a taste in my mouth, something like loneliness,
And watching my shadow reminds me
Along with the shivers.
But I don't mind it, really—
Do you think you would?
Maybe if it were every night, maybe your veins would scream aloud
And you'd listen to them as if they were voices
In the black, and you'd wonder
Who thought of street lights anyway.
How long are poems supposed to be, too, the midnight wanderer asks
As she approaches her door, or some semblance of it
I admit I am far from knowing, but please
If the poet may ask of anything,
Do not tell me.

Every glance is like a sting
Amidst the buzz of a crowded room
Or the bustling hive of forgettable faces,
I trace the scene until yours arises from the deep
Ocean swaying with laughs and chatter,
You are north and I am a magnet
Scaling the circle of the room
Like a compass
Looking in your direction.
The lazy sting returns, both sharp and silent
I want to walk toward you
I want to grab your hand
And take you somewhere
You can show me what the honey tastes like.

And I wonder if
In the moon's brilliance
It can even see
The seemingly dim stars;

I think they must be in love with it
    And it with the sun,
    Unrequitedly.

He is like mist,
Cool on the skin, and light in the air
Like a song;
He is the grass that grows,
Even between the cracks in the pavement.

Let the morning last
Into the afternoon,
The hazy daylight
Through the window
Is indifferent to us
What is a map, after all
But a false representation
Of where we must go—
Mercator, Mercator
There is only one place
I need be
So stay with me
Between these sheets
Trace down my longitude
And we'll live
Like it's still yesterday.

I will pose,
But I fear I cannot sit still—
For I live in motion, a film in fast-forward
Blurring between the lines of your strokes;
I wonder if you can catch glimpses of my silhouette, for what it is
Because the more I see of you, the more colors appear
You leave the impression
    Of water lilies,
Or the surrealism
    Of a daydream.
Anybody like me may stroll through your gallery,
Spending hours between its walls,
But in the midst of my wandering, you say you see
Something lovely in me,
Yet I wonder if that is only because
I walked by.

I write of you—
What is there to say of me?
I like how words sound
Together,
Like rain, falling
Together,
Like us.

He said he drifts out of himself
And into hazy thoughts of me,
Staring toward faraway places
Where I sit
Doing the same—
    Turning corners with white knuckles
    Laughing, I take your hand
    And look up to mock the sun
    While it vies for our attention
    With green, jealous leaves
    Giving us spots with their shadows.
        And then an evening without a moon
        To take the light
        From feeble, voiceless stars
        And we see an uprising of them
        Travel somewhere together
        In a flash like silk lightning.
            Finally,
            There is the dark
            But I see you clearly,
            Following the line of your jaw
            Down the curve of your smile
            And I know.
Suddenly I can hardly expect
Any more days without daydreams—
Oh, I'll be staring toward faraway places
Where he'll sit
Doing the same.

I need to see you
He said.
I should have told him
He can.

"Yesterday and tomorrow happen at once,"
I heard someone say once
And I believed it,
Living in between days as I pleased.

These stolen skies
Were somewhere behind the sun
But now hide in plain sight
Swirling around our heads.

I used to stay there,
Stuck
In freeze frames,
Memories like scratched CDs.

Now when I hear echoes
Of you
And you're not around
I let myself listen.

But I no longer sit
In dusty rooms
Gazing at faded shadows
Mouth words I don't remember.

There will be time
I tell myself,
And I spend it
There.

In the places we'll be.

Days pass,
I stand—
They stumble,
And I hardly hold on
While I swing between their steps.

Eyes closed
I feel for you,
And sigh without looking
For my love,
The mirage: the refraction.

The woman in love traces
A watery window with her finger,
Exposing the fog, denying translucency
The chance to cloud her vision.
Flushed, quiet, loud.
Have you seen her?

She sits in the middle of a hurricane,
The eye
At the center of turmoil
Pretending the world is at peace
While the winds howl and the waters rise
And she remains,
For her lover will find her there.
Have you seen her?

Expressions on her face
So carefully stitched to stupefy, and surrender
Quick glances in the voice of silent films
She beckons,
She calls.
Have you seen her?

There is something lovers say
About meeting halfway
And she, oh she believes it
Waiting, wishing, wanting.
Have you seen her?

Immaterial imaginings
Traced on the lines of your hand
Do we see what we crave
Or what we hate
In visions of ourselves—
In dreams?

How do we write
The past?
Fleeting sparks,
Somewhere between innumerable sunsets
And sunrises—
But memories are all sunsets,
Aren't they?
Obsessed with the close,
Monotonous and loud
In the moment, far away
I do not trust them.
The edges are blurred
In the photographs you see
Through rose-colored glasses
And kaleidoscope dreams
Of black and white scenes,
Forgive me,
But I know you, ghosts,
And tomorrow will long
For today just the same.

Walk sign is on for all crossings.
Walk sign is on for all crossings.

It's dark but it seems only dim now
The reds and greens throwing themselves at the street, like Christmas
Make your list and check it twice, yourself
For any errors;
Lick the envelope and it's yours.

Do people know what they're sure of
As clear as street-lights?
Or do they see something yellow when they close their eyes,
Like me,
Like anyone honest.

I wish it was five in the morning and no one was around but me
Pressing buttons, waiting
       Walk sign is on for all crossings.
But now it's colder than I thought
And I'm wondering if this was the best idea.

I just saw black masks color themselves in
Over the faces of some men
But I saw enough to recognize their eyes through the window
Wondering where I'm going all by myself—
At least they didn't whistle.

I am almost to where I'm going
And I think what I'm most afraid of is what to do
When there are no automated voices left
To tell me where to go, and no crowd
To fade into the next place with me.

Can others see me
Outside of themselves?
I think only God can,
But that does not demand
You miss everything,
And how lovely it is
To learn someone
Everyday.

Unearthed—
Like bones, fitting together
The deeper we go;
Or did we fall from the sky instead?
We are no Lazarus;
We needed not resurrection,
But a Big Bang
To set us into motion
At all, in the first place
And while you sleep
I lie, like those men
Who have looked up at the unanswerable sky
For centuries, wondering where they came from,
Because anything that exists begs the question,
From where, and how,
Is this real?
Oh, but why ask?
I am only glad that it is.

How do I write a person
Onto paper
When one cannot fit in the margins
Let alone in words
Tumbling on top of one another
Like the Tower of Babel
Stretching for heaven—
And falling short.

Did you ask me something?
I'm sorry, I was looking out the window
Wondering why pines don't lose their leaves in the cold,
And wondering if we are trees, too.
  When I was a kid I used to get sticky fingers
  On their trunks, thinking maybe it was maple syrup
  I could drip over my pancakes on a snow day.
  Are you ever sorry you'll never feel that way again?
  Oh, but love feels like angels we make on our own, in the snow
  Lying on our backs in the shape of stars
  As if they'd look down at us while we admire them—
  Do you think that they do?

You're behind the wheel
Because I hate to drive in the rain
But I love to watch it stream down,
Dropping like slow tears on the windshield.
Beautiful tears, the same ones we fight
Ironically blinking way our bliss, and so
It is there, in the red blur of the stoplight's tears
          Where I say it out loud.

What are you thankful for, my dear
They ask around the table once a year, or occasionally
In some sort of conversation about how the rain
Chose not to spoil our plans,
How lovely, the most wonderful thing
    Could we dare tell them what we lock our hands for
    In the night, before sleep?
    When we're allowed to think of anything, without distraction
    From the cracks in the wall, or the pills on the table
    Take me, they yell, Monday, Tuesday, everyday
    And you wonder whether or not you remembered—
    No, in the dark I am the most free
    My mind takes a deep breath, and exhales
    His geography, yes, directions
    Of where my mind would like to go, if it could choose,
    And I smile to myself, knowing this is love,
    When the most beautiful thing I could imagine,
    Without distraction, Monday, Tuesday, everyday
Is you.

I am a moonbeam
With silent rays
You cannot feel,
But see whisper along
The lines of others' faces
Like gossip.
Do you think they look
For me?
Or only for what I show them?

There is something in the lines of walls
Where one starts and another ends;
I run my finger along in expectation
       Of the turn, the bend.

In truth I ache to outline it all,
       Even the sound of you speak;
       And I memorize the shape of your shadow
       As it lingers across your cheek.

Look up from your plate and lift your glass
       I'm making a toast to the one I miss,
       That there is no room to enclose us
       And we run on and on just like this.

I speak because I feel unknown
And wish to pull my voice from my chest and into the air
For you to breathe in and taste on your tongue
Melting like snowflakes of sounds—gone just as quickly.

And sometimes I speak only because I'd like you to stay;
In a tender standoff, you listen until I give up—
Maybe that's why I do it, letting my voice fade on its own
Into the sharper thoughts of how I feel for you, I lose the words.

Then I cannot speak.

The good rests in the lines
And the bad in the prose on the other end;
Can the beautiful things you hear be what you believe, too,
Or may Vision adopt the dim?
My eyes are accustomed to the sun,
I welcome the blindness they speak of along with it,
For I'd like to see every bit of you, if I can,
In the light
Like that Led Zeppelin song, from *Physical Graffiti*,
And in the same way, you may write on me
If you'd like,
Fingers tracing my skin with ink,
And I'll smile and scrub it off my arms, all the while
Hoping I won't be able.

You told me the lashes of my eyes were like the rays of the sun;
I bet you think I was too drunk to remember—
No, but I was enough to wonder if that meant that looking at them hurt,
Silly;
But sometimes we convince ourselves of things we would hate to be true
Like pinching yourself in a dream, maybe
I take my skin between my fingers or bite my lip
To make sure that it isn't pretend,
And I hope you'll forgive me when I do it,
Because sometimes it can be difficult to know what's real.

In the earliest of mornings our eyes adjust to each other's outlines
I see you in the stripes of light peeking through the blinds
Stretching their fingers through the window and into our little room,
Curious to know the secrets we keep from the day—
Are secrets born when the two find it on their own
Or when others begin to notice its existence?
I think ours belongs to us because it is not shared by whisper-able words
Or cryptic codes in stamped folders, but rather
A feeling we never asked for, or even sought out in the first place,
Yet I thank the sun for it, in the morning—
Perhaps the reason it so desperately hopes to rise and see it too.

I felt words
Like emotions
    They stung.
    They ached.

I thought them loud,
Like reality
    They breathed.
    They screamed into microphones.

I would try and mold them, the artist's
Fingers breaking in pulls of unruly clay,
Like reckless teen spirit
Keeping secrets from the one who birthed it.

Now: I try and write of you
But my vision clouds its edges,
More vivid than this,
And much more beautiful, my dear.

I am bored with love, the word
And the way it sounds coming off my lips,
Like flimsy paper notices
Piled up on someone's desk,
In or out, back and forth
I'll stamp my signature for you.

I wait for a different word to come up, bobbling on the surface—
But these heavier things are not quite buoyant,
And sometimes I whisper your name
With nothing waiting in between my lips
Besides those sunken feelings, so joyous
I wish you could dive down with me.

And yet I must say it
Because without it what else would I utter
Besides hellos that only beg for no more goodbyes,
Still now I'm left to wonder
What else can come out of such lips—
With duct tape over my mouth I shall write.

Come here,
So you may feel what I cannot say
For there are not the words anymore,
Even for the one with all the letters stuck in her tongue
Tasting things by how they sound on the page--
I wish I knew how to say you out loud.

I stay up nights to sketch you with my pen
Scribbling out the errors of my unsteady hand, tracing your lines
Onto a page somehow—
We love art because it tries to tell us it loves us, too
And I suppose all I want is to draw your countenance
So it may belong to me, also.

www.ingramcontent.com/pod-product-compliance
Lightning Source LLC
Chambersburg PA
CBHW060545030426
42337CB00021B/4445